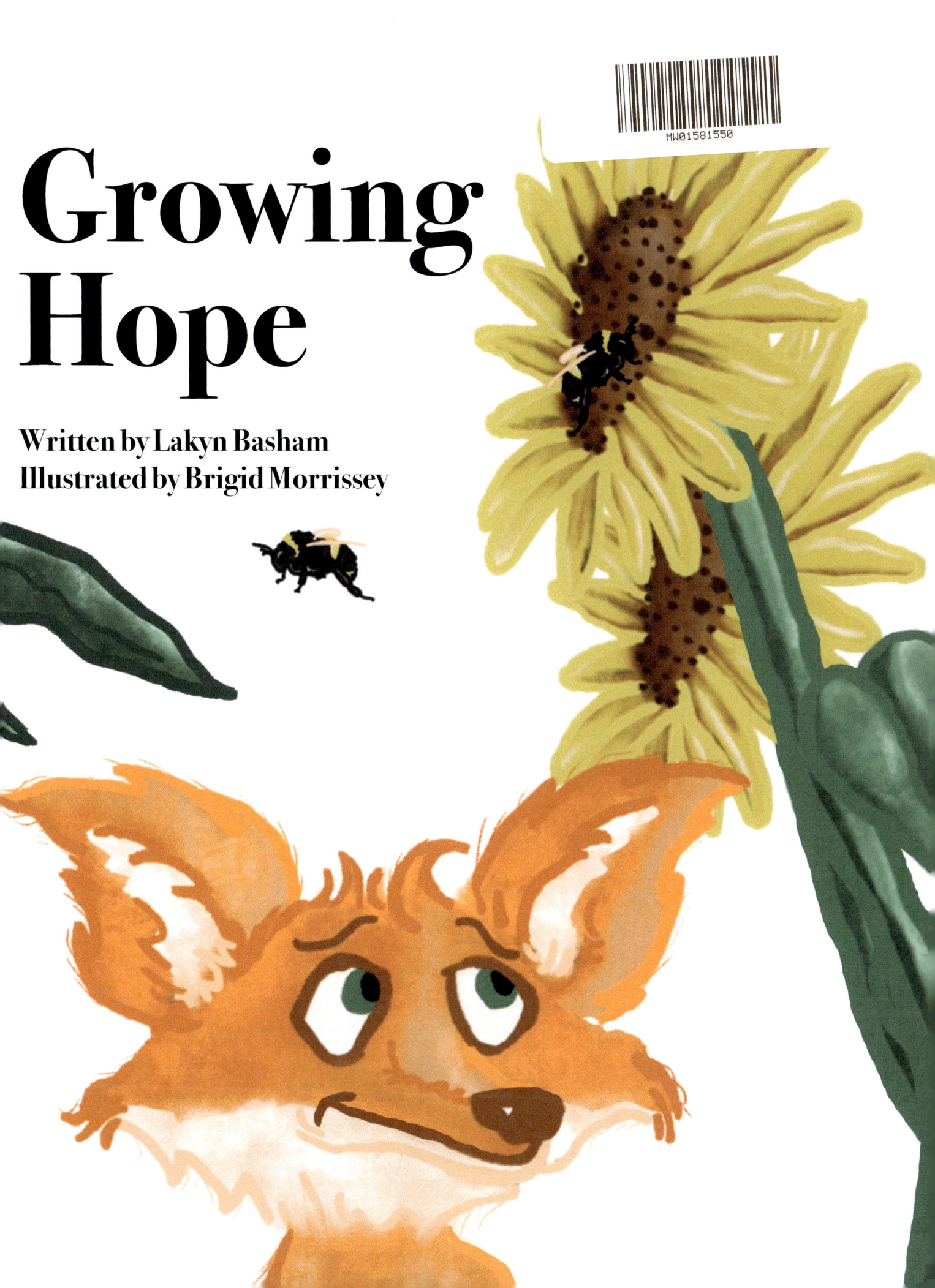

Growing Hope
Copyright © 2022 Lakyn Basham
All Rights Reserved

This is a work of fiction.
All rights reserved. This book or any portion thereof may not be reproduced, distributed, or transmitted in any form or by any means, including photocopying, recording, or other electronic or mechanical methods, without the express written permission of the publisher except in the case of brief quotations embodied in critical reviews and certain other noncommercial uses permitted by copyright law.
For permissions requests, write to the publisher, addressed
"Attention: Permissions Coordinator," at the address below.

Printed in the United States of America
ISBN: 978-1-953497-42-0 (Paperback)
ISBN: 978-1-953497-43-7 (Digital)
Library of Congress Control Number: 2022921949

Published by Cocoon to Wings Publishing
7810 Gall Blvd, #311
Zephyrhills, FL 33541
www.CocoontoWingsBooks.com
(813)906-WING (9464)

Illustrations and interior layout design by Brigid Morrissey/Cloud Atlas, LLC

Growing Hope

Written by Lakyn Basham
Illustrated by Brigid Morrissey

Lots of critters in my neighborhood have gardens.

Some are small and some are big, but my garden is extra special.

My garden is *magical.*

We start our garden once the earth starts warming back up.

I don't like the cold season. Everything seems dead and it is hard for me to see any magic.

Mama says the magic is there. It just looks different.
Things aren't dead. They are just sleeping.

Nature is showing us how important it is to rest. If we keep producing all the time, we end up shriveled and weak. Resting for a season helps us come back healthier and stronger.

Some days, I feel like the cold will never end and
we will never get to start our magical garden.

Times like this, my mind likes to play tricks on me.
It wants me to give up hope.

When it is hard to hold onto my hope, Mama is there to help.
She tells me everyone needs someone to hold their hope for them occasionally.

To help me, we focus on the fun days ahead.
Right now may seem bad, but better days always come.

This morning, the ice crystals on the grass have been replaced with little buds of yellow. The daffodils are waking from their long nap and are the first to welcome Spring.

I know it is time to get our garden started.

Mama uses the plow and turns up the dirt.
I pick up the hoe and rake the lines where the seeds will drop.

Getting the dirt ready isn't much fun but deep inside, I feel good.
I know I can do hard things. Now our garden is ready for the seeds.

I tear open the little seed packets and peek inside.
I see big gray seeds with white edges. These are sunflower seeds!

Mama says that to plant them, I need to let one seed fall from my hand every three steps.

If the seed never falls, it will never grow. Sometimes when I mess up, Mama reminds me that we are like seeds too.

We have to fall every once in a while, in order to keep growing into who we are supposed to be.

After all the seeds have been dropped, I get to tuck them in. I sing bedtime songs to my seeds and gently pull the dirt over them like Mama pulls my blanket up over me each night.

Each day after I plant the seeds, I run to our garden to
see if any green is poking through the dirt. Each day
I leave disappointed because I don't see anything.

Mama says waiting makes the magic even more special when it comes.
I still don't like waiting though.

There are a lot of boring, rainy days, but the sun always comes out after. Mama says it takes times of rain and sun for mighty things to grow. Sometimes we have to go through good and bad days to grow too.

After ten long days, I notice little sprouts pushing through the soil.

Before I know it the plants are as tall as me!

Our garden has become one of my favorite places to explore.
I like to pretend the sunflowers are castles.

I am a knight, and the bumble bees are dragons protecting a wizard inside.

I walk into the towering plants and feel so small. Mama reminds me that it is good to feel small every now and then. It helps you remember your part in the world. Things will feel really big sometimes. It is easy to get overwhelmed.

When you go somewhere that makes you feel small, nature reminds you that the world doesn't rest on your shoulders. If you mess up, nature will keep being magical, and in the end, it will all be okay.

Today while Mama and I are pulling up weeds, I hear a rumbling noise. I wonder if my belly is growling. The rumbling sound happens again, but this time it is much louder. It's not my stomach. It is thunder.

I start to walk down my row towards Mama.
The sky turns dark and big raindrops start to fall.
I don't feel happy anymore in the garden. I feel scared.

What Mama does next shocks me. Instead of being upset or running away from the rain shower, Mama starts laughing as the raindrops hit her skin. She shouts "thank you" towards the sky. She even dances a little!

As Mama twirls in the rain, I slowly feel my body relax.
Fear starts to leave my belly. I notice that the rain feels
like little tickles on my skin, making me giggle.

After we play in the rain for a while, we find shelter.
Mama says the rain taught us an important lesson.

In life it helps if you learn to embrace what you can't control.
We couldn't stop the rain so why not find a way to enjoy it?

After the storm passes, Mama and I go out to see
how much damage has been done to our garden.

Our castle sunflowers look like they have been trampled
by a giant dragon. Tears start filling my eyes.

I walk down the first row in our garden. When I get to the knocked down sunflowers, I begin finding ways to prop them up.

I notice Mama watching me.
It looks like there are tears in her eyes now.
After I stand up the last flower, my paws
covered in mud, I go to check on Mama.

When Mama saw a lot of our flowers knocked over, she figured they would die. She gave up hope for our sunflowers. So today, I held hope for Mama.

I knew some of our garden was destroyed, but there were some flower stalks that were only bent, not broken. It wasn't good, but it could have been worse.

Eventually our sunflowers start to rise on their own, standing tall with fresh hope and a new start, just like we get to do if we ever feel down.

I'm learning that even when there seems like there's no hope, there's always hope somewhere.

You may have to work through some dirt and weather a few storms. There will be hard work you'll want to skip, and you may have to get your hands muddy. But hope is there.

My garden is magical.
Not because it has castles or dragons or wizards.

It is magical because of what it teaches me without saying a word. It is magical because while I am growing seeds in it, it is growing hope in me.

Just because you don't see hope
Doesn't mean it isn't there
Look carefully or you'll miss it
Like a dragonfly in the air

Go back to the beginning
Search all throughout this book
To find 10 little dragonflies
That remind you to give hope a second look.

Lakyn Basham lives in a small town in Tennessee with her husband and two daughters. Together, they enjoy exploring the world around them and sharing their love for nature.

Her time in the garden started as a hobby, but quickly turned into some of the sweetest memories shared between her and her daughters.

She believes children and nature offer some of the best lessons, so spending time in her garden with her girls is a glimpse of heaven.

Brigid Morrissey resides in a sleepy southern Indiana town where she spent her childhood imagining and creating through all kinds of mediums.

She graduated from college with a BA in Studio Art and a concentration in Graphic Design, and has put it to use as a freelancer. She and her dad also own and operate The Root, a coworking space in their historic downtown.

Through her platform as a business owner, Brigid fuses her passions for art and connecting others to bring light to the world around her.

For Cana and Haven
Thank you for bringing so much hope into my life.

Made in the USA
Middletown, DE
02 February 2024

49006110R00029